Writings, Ramblings, and Rutabagas

Dennis Sorensen

Aakenbaaken & Kent

Writings, Ramblings, and Rutabagas

ISBN: 978-1-958022-12-2

Dedication

To Bobbie,
my soul mate and inspiration.

Table of Contents

Prose

Poetry

And a bit of both prose & poetry

Prose

*T*he Biggest Ball of String

A Driving Miss Bobbie Adventure

We like to drive. Actually, that is not accurate. We, using Bobbie's favorite multi-purpose and oft used verb, "LOVE" to drive.

During the fifteen-years we have been together, "who's going to drive first has been the cause of most of the disagreements we have had.

We have driven the 3,000 miles across the United States five times from Stockton to Beaufort, North Carolina and three times from Stockton to Davenport Iowa to visit kids, Grandkids, a great grandson, and many friends. It's a 4,000 plus mile round trip.

The Spam Museum in Austin. Minnesota was a hoot, as was the

Grotto in Dickey Ville, Illinois.

We have traversed the entire length of I-5 from San Ysidro to Vancouver, British Columbia (1,381 miles), and while living in the East we've driven the Atlantic Coast from Boston to Key West twice.

But it was after a three week vacation in Beaufort, North Carolina that we determined it was time for a real adventure. After an election ending in two yes; zero no, we decided to" do the deed" and make the move. Our California kids bought into our adventure and backed us One-hundred percent. After hugs, kisses and a few tears, we wished them well and would see them in a year. If they decided to visit us in North Carolina, we would see them sooner.

We sold both our homes in Stockton, gave all our furniture and household goods to charity, (The kids neither wanted nor needed our 40-year-old possessions). We packed "Vicky" the Crown Victoria, and "Cammy" the Camry to the gunnels with what was left: clothes, drugs, (the legal ones prescribed or bought over the counter), from cosmetics, toiletries, a couple of picture albums, a few family photos, a coffee grinder, Mister Coffee, and our indispensable cast iron skillet. Then at 6:00 AM on January 1, 2012, we watched Stockton recede in the rear view mirror as we headed to our new life in Beaufort, North Carolina.

A Driving Miss Bobbie

Adventure

(continued)

The Biggest Ball of String

Driving Rules:
No more than two hours per shift
Start early
Don't let the gas gauge get below
half full

On The Road Again

After deciding who drives first, off we go. No adventure too small. "Flying J", "Loves", "T/A Travel Stops", "Pilot Truck Stops", are adventures in and of themselves. Competitively priced gas, always a squeegee, and plenty of paper towels to clean the windshield. A scraper in case it's icy, clean rest rooms, and really good coffee. They also have sit-down restaurants with booths and a counter. Sometimes with a jukebox! Your food and drink requests are seen to by waitresses and waiters (no servers here). Most are middle-aged or older with names like, Flo, Dixie, Edie, and Butch.

The places are full of interesting people; those who drive for a living, those who drive for pleasure, those who make a living walking the massive parking lots and way too many, who for a multitude of reasons live in their vehicles.

They greet you with a "Hi, how's it goin'? Where ya headed? "Did you guys see the antelope a couple of miles back?"

These are fascinating people whom we respect and enjoy.

While driving, if we happen upon a billboard advising us that to see the "World's Biggest Ball of String, take exit number 127 on your right and drive 3.5 miles," you can bet your bottom dollar we're gonna take it.

"You can drive from here, Dennis, I'm tired."

Love to all, y'all.

Denny the Dane

*T*he Move to Beaufort

One of the necessities for our big move to North Carolina was medicine, both OTC and prescription. Since both of us were well over 65 we had enough meds to fill both a kit and a caboodle.

I packed all of mine in a plastic shoebox with a Snap-On lid. I found among my prescriptions a powerful narcotic that had been prescribed for my son who had moved out of the house more than a year ago. Knowing that I shouldn't throw it in the garbage or flush it down the toilet and not having time to take it to the drugstore for proper disposal, since it was 12:45 AM and we had both cars packed to the gunnels and planned to leave at 6 AM, I put it in my medicine box, put the box behind the driver's seat and forgot about it.

Both cars were packed as neatly as possible. Trunks, backseats, front passenger seats, the floor boards behind the front seats and the passenger seats floors. We made sure that the windows were not covered and that both the rearview and side mirrors gave us a safe view of our surroundings.

Bobbie had a front seat passenger –. a 2½ foot tall whimsical metal sculpture made of garden tools and painted red, yellow and black. His name was, and still is, Sheffield. He got lots of attention and rightfully so.

We had planned to take I-80 East but the highway through Flagstaff, Arizona had been closed for days and was expected to remain impassable for the better part of another week due to icy conditions. Therefore, our best option was the southern Route, I-10 East.

We spent the first night in Bakersfield then on to El Paso, Texas. We awoke from a good night's sleep at a Comfort Inn to find it had snowed during the night and the cars resembled great big snowballs. We started the cars, turned the heaters and defrosters on full blast and used plastic scrapers to clear the windows.

After it finally stopped snowing, and the highway had been cleared and salted, we felt it was safe to drive. We were once again on our way. We had gone just a few miles when another fast moving storm forced us to pull off the highway into a turn out.

I cleared the stuff from my passenger seat and made room for Bobbie. We huddled under blankets and pillows again for an hour or two until the weather front passed.

Our rule of never letting our gas tanks reach less than one-half full proved to be a blessing. Off we went with Bobbie in the lead. (By the way, I-10 across Texas is 837-miles and Bobbie thought the 80-mile an hour speed limit was the best thing about Texas.). The weather cooperated and we began to relax.

Soon we came upon a State of Texas Immigration Station where we endured a major trial on our East bound odyssey. It's funny now, but wasn't then. Bobbie after showing her driver's license, and a cursory check of her car whom she lovingly called "Vicky", was waved thru.

Me, not so easy!

After a few minutes of I.D. and registration examination, and "dog sniffing" (the biggest German shepherd I'd ever seen), I was asked politely but sternly to pull off into a parking area next to the Immigration Service Office.

"Please give me your car keys, Sir!"

"Please step out of the vehicle, Sir!"

These commands were giving me pause for thought.

"Please have a seat inside the office, Sir!"

What the hell is all this about, I wondered.

I looked out the window and saw the dog doing nuts sniffing in the open trunk and barking loudly while pawing through the packed back seat, fixing on my medicine box. An officer pulled out the box and brought it into the office. He handed me my son's meds, and in a particularly accusatory voice, barked, "What's this and who is Mark Sorensen"?

After explaining why I had packed it, he "realized" me as he pronounced it, but not before a lecture and one more shot to show me who was boss.

"Your eyes are bloodshot and your nose is dripping. Have you been smoking weed"?

Two more minutes explaining I was from Fresno and had hay fever all my life, hence the bloodshot eyes and running nose, then he finally said, "You're free to go".

Wow! Welcome to Texas!

*T*he Saga of the Danish

Coconut

(Sagaen om den danske kokosnød

This storey dates from the early 9th century C.E. when "Airwick the Malodorous", son of "Airsick the Barfer" and his Armada of two longboats, crewed by 27 Danish Vikings, one Swede, and Helga, having grown tired of raiding the British Isles and eating mutton, shepherd's pie, bangers and mash, and watercress sandwiches with no crusts, sailed out of Jutland turned Southwest and arrived at what is now known as Panama on what was called, "Ithmas" Day by Sarthia, Airwick's lisping navigator.

They enlisted the help of a

local midwife named Carmen, who was subsisting on unemployment benefits due to the lack of children being born to the local women. This was because all of the Panamanian females of child bearing age were suffering from the "No Yen To" virus and had no interest whatsoever in sex.

Carmen's sense of smell had left her after years of delivering babies from mommies who did not bathe on a regular basis. As a consequence, she had no problem, at all, with the likes of Airwick and his motley crew.

Since the canal would not be built for another eleven hundred years, the Vikings were forced to portage. And portage they did – for a Fifth Night. That's about 17½ days.

Then they sailed across Lake Gautun (or Gitchigumbee as it was known to the indigenous Panamanians)

They somehow got lost and ended up in Tijuana where they attended a dog race and a pony show.

The crew dined on fish tacos and soaked in *El Lago Aqua Caliente*. They lost track of Airwick for almost forty days because he had become clean and they were unable to smell his whereabouts.

Jumping ahead in our story; our *Flotilla Poquito* landed on the Beach at Waikiki but didn't stay long.

They were given copies of the Book of Mormon signed by Joseph Smith and noticed a golden statue of a guy playing a trumpet standing atop a grass hut. Airwick and crew left without discovering what the hard broken cups were that the L.D.S. folks required the Hawaiian women to wear to cover their beautiful breasts.

They sailed Southwest where they saw the Southern Cross for the first time and ended up on a very, very strange island with weird stone statues even weirder, (or if you prefer, more weird) animals, and a white guy named Darwin.

The place was inhabited by a race of handsome well endowed people. On this island grew a very singular tree. The Vikings had seen a tree growing in Brooklyn on a previous trip from Reykjavík to Labrador via New York City.

This tree, however, was an anomaly; only one foot in circumference but 164 feet high with bushy, bushy green fronds now. It was called a Beach Boy tree.

Why I Like Mornings

Geese flying over the house just before dawn. In formation. Honking!

Why?

Who cares? It's wonderful.

Their cousins – wrens, jays, sparrows, robins, mocking birds, hawks and occasional turkey vultures are busy with life, and I get to enjoy their songs, sounds and their being.

No wake-up calls for me. My little mind knows when it's time to rise, shine, and embrace the day. I get up early to make the most of it. I brew the coffee, Swiffer the tile floor, empty the dishwasher, bring in the paper, (maybe start the crossword), take out the trash and attend to my morning ablution.

I check out yesterday's To-Do List and consider how to get the things done that didn't get done.

Yes. Then, of course, I start my list for today.

I take my morning pills and inject my insulin thankful that I can afford these life-sustaining meds.

Bobbie and I usually take time to talk about the up-coming day, what happened yesterday, and lots of other stuff. However, this does not happen until she checks out the "Obits" and we have our first cup of New Mexico Piñon coffee and a bit of breakfast.

Where, oh, where has the morning gone? I now have a 12 to 14-hour recess before bedtime.

Morning has broken!

$\mathcal{T}$he Dark Knight

It was a dark and swarmy knight who sat astride his gelded steed, Tea Biscuit, who led a motley band of varlets, knaves and random sorts through Cunningham Forest in pursuit of Ritchie, Mr. "C", and de Fonz, the usurpers of Good King Richard III's crown and kingdom.

"Fie! Fie! A pox upon those who would overthrow our liege", shouted Friar Chuck. "Let us not tarry in this place for I spy with my own bloodshot eye light appearing thru yonder thicket. It cometh from the east where a tavern be as well as from where the sun also rises. My throat is parched and I would quaff a pint or two."

"Two or four or maybe more" agreed Little Juan (Chuy) Valdez who had, only yesterday joined the merry band, having become weary picking hops sixteen hours a day as part of the bracero program.

The Cunninghams taxed the poor without mercy. When the serfs couldn't pay up, the Cunninghams foreclosed and deeded the property to their rich and powerful friends.

The oppressed were forced to work for peanuts which were in short supply as most were in storage silos in Georgia under the watchful eye of George "Goober" Lindsey and the Bush family who were awaiting their annual government subsidy check before releasing the legumes for export.

What to do, what to do?

"I have it" exclaimed the Dark Knight.

"Try penicillin" suggested Alan-a-Dale.

"It worked when I had it."

"No, you dolt!" I have an idea!

"I will issue a challenge to the

Cunninghams, a game of Jacks. Me against their chosen best. Winner take all!"

"What's all?" Asked Friar Chuck.

"A laundry detergent," the knight answered, "Something of which we've not availed ourselves."

"The prize must be one that both sides covet and it is a contest that we must win. The kingdom must be preserved!" chimed in the winsome Maid Marion. "I am willing to be that prize."

The challenge was issued and terms of victory agreed upon.

The winning side would be in control of all King Richard's "Land and Chattel" in perpetuity plus three years.

The competing sides picked their champions.

The Dark Knight vs. LeFonz.

The champion would be dubbed a monarch and spend a fortnight in the chambers of the fair damsel.

Let the games begin!!

Jacks it was. Best four out of seven.

Drummers drumming
Pipers piping
Ladies dancing
Laddies dancing
Lassies prancing
Geese a laying etc., etc.

In the shag of the night 'neath the full moon's pure light and a good sized bonfire, with the entire shire in attendance, the Games they did begin.

And went on and on as the cock crowed to greet dawn.

The game was tied at three.

Then, LeFonz's jack got stuck in a crack and he was unable to score.

It was up to the Knight and he did it alright and the crowd gave one heck of a roar!!!

The good did prevail,
The bad landed in jail

And the dish ran away with the spoon.

The Dark Knight spent his well-earned two weeks in the tent of she who had promised herself to the victor.

All that time in the sack
Caused a massive attack
A six on the scale of Richter

The funeral was held in the Great Hall of Nottingham Cathedral with buttressed walls and tintinnabulation tower.

Yes, his life here was through but everyone knew that the Dark Knight had truly made Marion.

Where, oh where, have my glasses gone?

And other things as well?

I read a lot of books, newspapers, magazines, mail, stuff on the computer, etc.

I use non-prescription reading glasses. I have seven or eight pair in strengths from 2 to 3.5.

The other morning I went outside at 6 am to bring in the newspaper. It was raining.

Hallelujah!

I came back in, tossed the paper on the kitchen table, drank my obligatory 24 ounces of water and sat down at the table to read the *Record* and work on the crossword.

H'mmm, no readers. The search was on.

No readers on the bed side

table where I had left a pair after reading a couple of chapters of a mystery novel before going to sleep.

I scoured both bathrooms, the dining room table, the side table in the music room, under the bed and on the top of the writing desk, where the computer lives.

To the garage to search the cars. Finally under the seats, in glove compartments, consoles etc., I found seven pair. I should be okay for a few days.

I put on a pair of 2.5 's, opened the paper to page 8b which contained the crossword, puzzle and reached for a ball point pen. Yes, I use a pen.

No pen!

After uttering a couple of epithets, unfit for my great-grandson's ears, I headed for the writing desk, where the computer lives.

There, in a 'kqed" mug, designated for use as a pen, pencil, ruler holder, were thirteen pens, eight pencils, a black marks-a-lot, six rubber bands, and a partridge in a pear tree.

The whereabouts of my cell phone is, and always has been, a source of irritation and embarrassment.

I've lost it in both cars. Under the seats, on the seats, between the seats as well as on the floor.

The floor is black, the seats are black, my phone is black.

Sometimes it hides in plain sight- like on top of the writing desk, where the computer lives.

The rascal has almost always been found by having Bobbie call it with her phone.

But one time, a couple years ago after a search lasting about a day and a half, I decided to search the trash cans, just in case.

They were lined up in the street, since it was Wednesday morning and the garbage trucks would soon arrive.

Nothing in the green waste can; nothing in the black can.

Bobbie called my phone one more time. It rang from inside the yellow lidded can just as the truck arrived to haul it away.

I yelled at the driver and waved my arms to no avail.

The last I saw, or rather, the last I heard of my phone was its ring tone tumbling down, down, down into the bowels of the big blue Republic Sanitation truck.

So off to Verizon to buy a new one,

$\mathcal{P}$oems

Alphabet Soup

From A to Z
Z is for Zeppelin, it's so full of gas

Y Is for Year, and it too shall pass

X Is for Xylophone, where you can play scales; it's also for Xanadu - what wondrous tales

W Is for Wort, used to make ales

V Is for Vying; that's someone who's trying

U Is for Up, a direction to go

T is for Treadle, a machine that can sew

S Is for Syzygy, a word with three Y's

R Is for Rhino, they're big for their size

Q Is for Quack, the sound of a duck

P Is for Pixie - some bring us good luck;

O Is for Oxtail; the bone makes

Dennis Sorensen 46

good soup

𝒩 Is for Nomads, a wandering group

𝓜 Is for Mule, a horse and a donkey; trying to rhyme this is driving me Wonky

𝓛 Is for Loblolly, a thick gruel or a Pine, it's also for Lucifer whose place is behind

𝓚 Is for Kink that's a twist or a curl, and also for kiss and that's fun with your girl

𝒥 Is for Jumper, it's something to

wear; it's also for jinx, of which you should beware

I Is for Igloo, a house made of ice, and also for instant, like Uncle Ben's Rice

H Is for Hussy and men would be wise to keep their hands off and go home to their wives

G Is for Goldfish, they live in a bowl and also for geyser; it spouts steam from a hole

F Is for French Cuff at the end of your sleeve, or it might be for frigate that sails on a breeze

E Is for ESSO, a Canadian gas and also for Emu; they run really fast

D Is for Dirk, a long skinny dagger, or maybe for Double, a baseball 2-bagger

C Could be for Confidence (stick your chest out and strut) for sure it's for Cur, a scraggly old mutt

B Is for Brussels, a green tender sprout and also for badges worn by a scout

A Is for "All done", so say "Holy Cow!"
Alleluia, amen; it's over for now.

This lexiconic exercise was brought

to you by Denny the Dane and Noah
Webster

Dennis Sorensen 50

*A*vocadoes

Not an original thought…
But at three in the morning
When I can't sleep
It's one I think about a lot

Good ones can cost two dollars or
more
Squishy ones two bits
A question came into my mind just
now
Do they ever have two pits?

And if they had…
Would it be so bad?
If one was named Zasu
The other one Brad.

It's three-twenty seven
In my slumber I wonder
Does avocado like Avogadro
Have a mind-boggling number?

ℋair and other Miseries

Some guys have too much hair
In their ears and on their backs
The top of their heads
Now that's where it lacks

Many men shave two, three, four times a
day
Just to keep five o'clock shadow at bay

At times hair grows thick
In the nose and the toes
Why does this happen
Do you suppose?

Some gents are bald
And save money on cuts
Some don't don Bikinis
'Cause' of big hairy butts

God did this to men
And because God is fair
Did the same to women
But they can use Nair

—Lenny Mcdennis,   Oct. 2022

53 Writings, Ramblings, and Rutabagas

The Tree

There was an old woman

Who lived in a tree

She dina come down

Not to poop, nor to pee

Her kin had all moved

To houses nearby

And nary a one

Could fathom just why,

On a crisp Christmas Eve

A decade ago,

Granny McDermott

Decided to go,

"For a walk" she said

As she jumped from her bed

While visions of a sort

Raced thru her head

"She's always been crazy"

Said her daughter named Sue,

Her nephew dubbed Gregor

Said he thought so too!

The entire raucous clan

From the Isles had come,

The praties don't grow

But Scots they're not dumb

So New Scotia was where

They decided to go.

Bairns and parents,

Grans and greats,

Packed up their meagers,

And trusting their fate

To God up in heaven,

They boarded the ship

At aalf past eleven.

Dennis Sorensen 56

New life had begun

For the four generations,

Plenty of food

And lots of libations,

One bonny wee lassie

Whose name was Nell,

Moved into the house

Where granny did dwell

'til gran decided

To live in the tree.

The clan was now led

By "Lennie the Bruce",

Who'd stowed away on the boat

To escape the noose.

{This thing is sounding a little like

Seuss}

Lenny had been accused

Of writing and reciting

Off color limericks

And off color rhymes.

He decided at once

What had to be done

Go visit granny

While there was still sun

So out to the yard

As quick as could be

Sixty-five people

Looked up to see

If the crazy old woman

Was still in the tree

"She's up there, I see her"

One of them said

The kin folk were thankful

That she wasn't dead.

Her coat was less white,

Her dress was less red,

Her beautiful smile

Left naught to be said

For Granny McDermott

Found peace, don't you see?

There was no earthly reason

To come down from her tree.

Dennis Sorensen 60

TickleTime

Scuttledooley Lampsalot
Little Pinky Slickapot
Lucy is a pepper shaker
Drop her and you just might break
her

Black and White and Read all over
Looking for a four leaf clover?
Maybe there's a cat named Rover
Chalky like the cliffs of Dover

Twirly Burley ankle sox
I've heard that Hoosiers don't like
lox
It says so on the corn flakes box.

Every stanza has to rhyme

Sitting here just killing thyme

Buggaty, Buggaty pills in a vial

Walk in others' shoes a mile

Exit through the wrong turnstile

Dirty clothes go in that pile

Stupider, Stupider, you can bet

This thing ain't nearly over yet

I know you really wish it was

So I'll continue just because . . .

I CAN !!!

Shorts Stories

Electrical Shorts

They keep your bottom and boys
warm
 But are limited by extension cord

length

 And outlet availability.

Boxer Shorts

Barbara wears them

And those drooling canines

Really have no way to drop them

Nor to pull them up before

Or after Frequent stops for #1

Up against a tree

Or #2 on your neighbor's lawn.

Y-Fronts

They let you keep your belt buckled

When using a urinal

Keeping your trousers up

So a guy can use both hands

Insuring proper aim

And letting said guy

Control his favorite tool

With his hand of choice

While using the other

To brace himself against the wall.

Briefs

Briefs are worn by attorneys

When preparing for a day in Court

and also for really, really short

People so their undies don't drag on

the floor.

Board Shorts

Board shorts are worn
By directors in a room,
Deciding by majority vote
What's to be done by whom?

Bikinis

Bikinis cover almost nothing
"Atoll".

Thongs

Thongs are worn at beach or pool,
Designed in fact to make men drool,
My duty is to bring to light
They cannot hide one's cellulite.

Bermuda Shorts

Pants that stop above the knees

Are named, it is surmised,

For an Atlantic Archipelago

That's not too big in size

They're unisex that is to say

For men and women too

And since I'm at a loss for words

I'm calling this rhyme through!

Ramblings of a

Sagittarian Octogenarian

3I was born eighty years ago
December 7, 1942.
One year after
"A Day That Will Live in Infamy".
An aging Sagittarian.
What if anything,
Does this mean?
I can do nothing about the past.
Poof! It's gone.

Tomorrow and tomorrow and tomorrow…
Time does not creep
Time passes in a flash

I try not to dwell on how many
Days, months, or years I have left.

Eighty Years!

What can I do to
Make the world a better place?
What can I do to help?

I know that I have been loved
I know that I am loved today

Not just be family, friends,
And old acquaintances,
But also by millions who keep good
Thoughts and, if so inclined,
Prayers for all creatures, great and small.

Let me not
Let them down

Dennis Sorensen 68

A Child's Thanksgiving

Rhyme

Remember it?

The Pumpkin ran away
Upon Thanksgiving Day
She said, "They'll make a pie of me"
If I should dare to stay

The turkey ran away
Upon Thanksgiving Day
He said, "They'll make a feast of
me" If I should dare to stay

Well, Bobbie and Dennis
Would have/should have run away
Before Thanksgiving Day
Shoulda, coulda, woulda…?
They decided to stay

Five adults from Brentwood
And one from Walnut Creek
Plus two great grandsons,
One and four
Both blonde with rosy cheek

About a million dollars
Was spent to decorate
The home, the yard, the vestibule
And, of course, the garden gate

Mrs. and Mr. Scarecrow
Each 'bout five feet tall
Greeting friends and passer's bye
From a niche within the wall

A twenty-one pound turkey,
Potatoes and gravy too
Would be prepared by us, the hosts
The least that we could do

The rest, the pies, the stuffing
As well as crudités
Would be supplied by guests
Whose names are Brown and Grey

Dennis Sorensen 70

A bowling set was in the hall
For all of us to play
Kids can stand as close as they want
The old folks, far away

Champagne on ice was there, of
course,
Juice and Pepsi too
A birthday cake for Wesley
Who was turning two plus two

Anticipation running high
We would shortly laugh and sing
Just two more hours so we thought
But then the phone did ring

The little ones both were sick,
Four of six adults as well
The party that was so well planned
Just got blown to Hell!

A question has just come to mind
And I trust it's not to crude
What in the world we're gonna do
With all this festive food?

Answer:
Carrie, Bobbie, and Dennis
Made eight meals to go
With zip-lock bags,
And paper cups
And plastic plates
And cling wrap too

Loaded it all in Carrie's van
And westward she did to!
Phew!!!

So much to be thankful for
Our gratitude abounds.
Hope your day was one of joy.

Winnie Baygo

Winnie Baygo lived to travel
Both on paved roads and on gravel
She minded chuck holes not a bit
For many miles she would sit
Take in the passing scenery
Of all the colors she beheld
Her favorite was the greenery

The asphalt black,
The lines of white
Were only there to guide her
Green grass, green trees,
Green frogs on logs
Continued to delight her

She sits upon the driver's seat
Made of leather only
There's no one to the right of her
You'd think that she'd be lonely
But no, she's not.

Her window is down
She waves to those she meets
Her destiny's to roam, you see
On highways and city streets

It's time to stop this silly rhyme
It's really time to quit
For Winnie loves to ride the road,
Let her get on with it!

Sequel

The time will come
Pray no time soon
When we end this tiny tome

And Winnie Baygo
Lies in bliss
'Neath the green, green grass of
home.

$\mathcal{P}$laces

I have not been to more places
Than I have been.

Places I have been:

Some were hot, some were cold
Some were new, some were old
Some were far some were near
Some served prune juice, some
served beer
Some were dry while some were wet
Some had no nurses, just a vet
Some had blue skies, some were
cloudy

Some were placid, some were rowdy
Some were fancy, some were dowdy
That's how places are

Places I have not been:

I haven't been to Mali
To visit Timbuktu
I haven't been to Alice Springs
To see a kangaroo

Iceland, Greenland, Nunavut
As well as Lake Baikal
They somehow still elude me
As does Kathmandu, Nepal

I haven't been to Mesquite, TX
To see a rodeo
I haven't been to Pompeii
To see the lava flow

I haven't been to Oedipus
To see mother lovin' Rex
I haven't been to Haiti
To take part in a hex

So many places yet to go
So many things to see
And I will be to many more
If time is good to me.

Dennis Sorensen 78

A mix of prose and poetry

$\mathcal{H}$ow boring was your day?

You hit the sack at eleven
And reflected upon your day
Was it great? Did it suck?
Or, like most days of late,
Was it kind of just okay?

You made your usual Costco list
Put new t/p on the spindle.
You considered calling your sister
But like gas
That thought soon passed.
Look at the time – only 9:42.
Turn on the telly to see what's new?
Or watch Whoopi on *The View*?
What to do? What to do?

Five years divorced, but you
don't need a man. You've already
rolled out the garbage can. So....
Costco it is. List in hand, off you go

to Lodi, wander around the store for an hour or so, fill up the cart, check out and head for the door.

You motor on back toward Stockton, not really too much of a chore, remembering to use Harney lane that'll get you home by four.

By the time you unload it and put it away, it's almost the end of your tedious day.

So back to the sack, perchance with dreams. Yes, your life really is as dull as it seems.

Costco?

Really?

You start to think about tomorrow. Maybe the drive-thru car wash is a possibility.

Acknowledgements

I wish to thank the members of the Olli writing group at the University of the Pacific: Annie, Bobbie, Brenda, Donna, Judy, Lise, Mary and Mel, my very best 99-year-old compadre.

And Mike Orenduff, my publisher and advisor for taking a chance on me.

CPSIA information can be obtained
at www.ICGtesting.com
Printed in the USA
BVHW041811170323
660665BV00010B/729